Music

MW01093357

History of Music: From Prehistoric Sounds to Classical Music, Jazz, Rock Music, POP Music and Electronic Music

information contained within this document, including, but not limited to, —errors, omissions, or inaccuracies.

Table of Contents

Introduction 5

Chapter 1 – The History of Modern Music..................8

Chapter 2 – The History of Classical Music................10

Chapter 3 – The History of Jazz and Blues................18

Chapter 4 – The History of Rock n' Roll 21

Chapter 5 – Country and Western Music 25

Chapter 6 – Electronic Music 26

Chapter 7 – Pop Music..28

Chapter 8 – Prehistoric Music and Instruments........29

Chapter 9 – Love of Music Explained........................36

Chapter 10 – Music in Modern Society 40

Chapter 11 – Folk Music in Europe, Asia, Africa and South America 46

Conclusion...53

Introduction

PROBABLY THE BEST BOOK CLUB ONLINE...

"If you love books. You will <u>love</u> the Lean Stone Book Club"

The Universal language of music can easily be understood by everyone, although all cultures have their own distinct forms of music, can transcend the boundaries and limitations of spoken and written language because it is based on people's feelings. Music often has a very powerful effect on people, throughout history, it has been used to indicate acts of friendship and love, but also aggression, used to send messages through time and space, record events, set the mood for gatherings and send messages long distances for example the Swiss yodel, African drums and the Australian Aboriginal didgeridoo and whispering sticks. Sometimes a natural form of music is created by using "wind chimes" and "dream catchers." Many animals also enjoy and react to music. If we find other life forms in the universe, it's likely that they will also understand it, leading to a method of communicating with them. Music is used for many reasons, to convey feelings and messages from one person to another, to give a feeling of peace and serenity, to communicate with spirits and in religious activities, to express the feelings of joy, wonderment, sorrow, and hope. Sometimes it is made for a small group and other times to connect with a large group. Before the formation of written languages, music and song was used to record events and pass down information through the generations. It is used in spiritual events, for healing, general entertainment and celebrations. All cultures around the world have their own unique form of music with as many variations as there are people belonging to those groups.

A world without music for me would be a barren place, music is used to enrich people's lives, bring comfort and emotional release as well as entertainment and relaxation. Many people listen to music for the sheer beauty they find in it; in our modern world, there are all manner of music styles available through many different outlets

This book will concentrate on our Modern style of music that most people in the western world recognize. To be sure that all the information is being seen for the important details of history, each chapter will have a quiz at the end. These quizzes will be short and for your own benefit as you will be able to go back and remember more information if needed. The answers to each of these quizzes will be found in the conclusion of the book.

Chapter 1: The History of Modern Music

Much of our modern music stems from around 500 B.C. when Pythagoras started to experiment with acoustics. The word music comes from the Ancient Greek muses, named after the nine goddesses of art and science. Music as we know it actually began during the Middle Ages as a Gregorian chant, named for Pope Gregory I. The monks in the Catholic Churches used it to enhance their services. This very early music mainly consisted of a variety of sacred Latin texts, sung without any instrumentation. Music was mainly in the churches until about the end of the Middle Ages; it started to become popular with wandering minstrels who would perform music and acrobatics in castles, taverns, and town squares.

By the about the 15th century or The Renaissance 1450-1600 period generally there was more importance placed on the words or lyrics than the instruments used, this style was called word painting, with the invention of the printing press. Written music was suddenly made available to many more people and an explosion of new composers began. Music was being written for pleasure, no longer confined to the church and nobility.

The people were more prosperous during the eighteenth century and wanted luxuries such as theater, literature, and music, which had a great impact on music with public concerts and the festivals.

From 1800 to 1900 there was a huge increase in the popularity of unique music styles that usually incorporated emotion and expression into the words, to follow a story, poem, idea, or scene. The instruments would be used to represent the emotions, characters, and events of a particular story, conveying the sounds and motion of nature, it is important that a composer obtained a specific mood or atmosphere for the audience to feel the music.

Beethoven was one of the first freelance musical composers; he inspired many others to freelance and compose for their own pleasure. The middle class was demanding more music, public orchestras, and operas became more popular, with Conservatories forming in the first half of the nineteenth century throughout Europe. In the United States music was also becoming increasingly more popular with conservatories opening in Chicago, Cleveland, Boston, Ohio, and Philadelphia during the late nineteenth century. A lot of composers created music for home use, as at this time many homes had pianos.

Quiz:

Question 1: What is word painting?

Question 2: What invention came around with the style of word painting?

Question 3: Who was one of the first freelance musical composers?

Chapter 2: The History of Classical Music

In the history of music, there is much that can be seen and much that can be learned. Through history by itself, there are multiple references and many places of experience that can be tied together in order to create a fellowship for the future to be built upon. In the history of classical music, it all begins in the different time periods where people used music for the purposes of religion and to be able to have entertainment. For the higher monarchs and the higher people of royalty, music was used to pass the time or provide another perspective as they were able to develop themselves through strategies in order to protect the land and the people around them.

At the start of the 1100's, people began by using chants to create different sounds and rhythms that people found pleasing. Just as people today follow through the rhythm and instrument of the music, it all started through the sounds of simple instruments coming together.

Modern classical music's origins can be traced back to a single line of notes known as the Monophonic chant which was developed in various church centers throughout Europe, with different styles coming from the different regions or countries such as France, Germany, Italy Portugal and Spain. Around 1011 A.D., when the Catholic Church became standardized through the two main European centers, Rome, the center of the church, and Paris, the political center, modern classical music began to take form.

The Medieval Period (1100-1400)

Two of the earliest known composers, Léonin and Pérotin, provided a variety of new compositional techniques, to the religious chant the most vital being modal rhythm, this was essentially irregular notes arranged in a regular pattern. Gradually more lines were introduced to the music as it evolved in such places the Florid Organum of St Martial and the famous Notre Dame School, leading the way for the music to lead to major/minor tonality.

The Renaissance Period (1400-1600)

During this period the music gradually became more complex with composers like Johannes Ockehem. The first impact of the printing press was felt in music around 1470's, allowing the reproduced of music and the further standardizing of music for a growing international market, with further refinements allowed both clarity and musical interest to develop.

This period's obsession with antiquity, in particular, the Greeks, leads some to the formation of musical theater, where a story was told accompanied by instruments, a form of musical theater that is still present today.

The Baroque Period (1600-1750)

During this period, the composer Jacopo Peri was, according to some, the true and original inventor of a new form of music called, Opera. Music from this area is thought to be some of music history's greatest masterpieces such as the music of Bach and Handel but at the time was considered to be overly ornamented and exaggerated.

The Classicism Period (1750-1820)

This is the time when people's taste in music was shifting from the very much respected Bach and Handel to the styles of Joseph Hayden and Wolfgang Amadeus Mozart. Hayden, who is often referred to as the father of both the String Quartet and the symphony had the benefit of a court appointment so had a good supply of musicians to work with. Mozart sought success within the public domain and would have had to hire musicians, which would mean rehearsals, and rehearsals cost money so, in order to limit the budget, pieces requiring only one rehearsal, became en vogue. He sold subscriptions to his concerts in order to finance himself, rather than relying on Royal patronage.

Both Hayden and Mozart were considered as geniuses at the time and enjoyed a great deal of success, Hayden composed over 100 symphonies, Mozart wrote 41, and Beethoven composed 9 symphonies.

Romanticism Period (1820-1900)

During this time of the middle classes new found prosperity and the development and interest in nature, the glorification of subjective thinking and the interest in the supernatural characterized the Romanticism. Musicians were finding it easier and were able to form more subjective approaches to their music they produced an array of popular free form styles such as nocturnes, rhapsodies, and preludes. Frederick Chopin incorporated elements of folk music in compositions, although he only gave a few concert performances as his usual income came from giving lessons and selling his manuscripts.

Wilhelm Richard Wagner pioneered compositions that were called The Total Art Work, or as he called them Gesamtkunstwerk, where in the poetic, visual, musical, and dramatic elements of art came together. Orchestras were growing larger and more complex at this time, with the introduction of more instruments and greater roles for existing ones.

Modernism, Serialism, and Beyond (1900)

The 20th Century saw huge changes in music many composers were looking for a change in direction, from The Phantom of the Opera a novel by French writer Gaston Leroux that was published in volume form in late March 1910 by Pierre Lafitte. A story partly inspired by historical events at the Paris and adapted as Andrew Lloyd Webbers 1986 Musical.

Now in the 21st Century, many believe we are experiencing a new wave of classical music from many diverse areas around the world. With the age of computers and social media being able to spread the idea and entertainment around the world instantly and at very little cost more and more people are finding out classical does not necessary mean stuff composed by long dead white guys. A few living and very productive and interesting modern classical composers that are making more than just a mark on society are:

Mark Anthony Turnage wrote an opera called Anna Nicole based on Anna Nicole Smith, Playboy Playmate, and tabloid darling. He also wrote Blood on the floor; this is about drug addiction mixing classical style with jazz.

Frederic Rzewski is an American composer who takes on big political topics such as his "Coming Together" that is based on letters by inmates from Attica State Prison during the riots therein. His most famous composition is "The People United Will Never Be Defeated" a piano composition.

Saed Haddad, a Jordanian composer now living in Germany has his music firmly rooted in his Arab upbringing; he often addresses cultural imperialism with his music.

He is a firm believer that music is the best vessel for sorting through your identity. He writes, "Like it or not; I definitely regret the present scenery of my Western culture." His music is a bold strike against the cultural closed-mindedness he sees all around him, and a celebration of his own culture (Bernier, 2016).

John Luther Adams is a well-known and accomplished naturalist composer. His music is inspired by (and sometimes performed in) natural landscapes, particularly the Alaskan environment where he lives. "Become Ocean" is a composition he wrote that won the 2014 Pulitzer Prize for music

Unsuk Chin, a South Korean composer is one of the most playful and versatile musicians in any genre her first opera was "Alice in Wonderland." She has won various awards, among them the esteemed Arnold Schonberg Prize. She mixes different styles of electronic and acoustic sounds

John Adams composition "On the Transmigration of Souls about 9/11 won the 2003 Pulitzer Prize for arguably the most important classical music composition of this century. He has nominated for this year's Pulitzer for a work called "The Gospel According to the Other Mary."

Johann Sebastian Bach (1685– 28 July 1750), a German composer and musician of the Baroque period is generally regarded as one of the greatest composers of all time, because of the technical command, artistic beauty, and intellectual depth of his music. He was born into a great musical family, which exposed him to much contemporary music, Johann Ambrosius Bach, his father was the director of the town musicians, and all of his brothers and uncles were professional musicians. His father probably taught him to play the violin and the harpsichord and his brother other instruments

He was highly respected organist during his lifetime and although he was not widely recognized as a great composer until a revival of interest in and performances of his music in the first half of the 19th century. After graduating from St. Michael's School, Bach served as the Director of Music to Leopold, Prince of Anhalt-Kothenand, also in Leipzig as music director at the main Lutheran churches, and as an educator. He received the title of "Royal Court Composer" from Augustus III in 1736 until his health and vision declined and he died.

Wolfgang Amadeus Mozart (1756 to 1791) was a musician capable of playing multiple instruments; he had learned to play the piano at 3 years old and started playing in public at the age of 6. Mozart composed hundreds of works over the years that included sonatas, symphonies, masses, concertos and operas. His work was notable because of the vivid emotion and sophisticated textures he incorporated into it.

Mozart's death came at a young age, even for the time period, he was only 35; yet he managed to be considered one of the greatest composers of all time. His music presented a bold expression, often times complex and dissonant, and required high technical mastery of the musicians who performed it.

Richard Wagner; Many people have claimed that Richard Wagner was "one of the most hateful and unpleasant people who ever walked the earth." Wagner despised Jews and blamed all the problems of the world on them. (Quizlet, 2016) Butfor all his prejudices, his music transcends all the idiocy of the man himself. He only wrote operas, which he termed "music dramas." Several of his finest masterpieces are Tannhauser, Lohengrin, in which you'll find the world-famous "Here Comes the Bride" theme, Tristan und Isolde, which many people consider his finest achievement, Die Meistersinger von Nurnberg, Parsifal, and his gargantuan four-opera cycle Der Ring des Nibelungen,

Wagner composed 7 of the longest operas known, four of them being the single most famous masterpiece in opera history, they had an average length of 3 hours, with Gotterdammerung, the last of the Ring cycle, 6 hours long. Wagner invented the leitmotif, a very short melody which represents a character, emotion, event, or object. Wagner revolutionized the art of opera, with almost all operas written in his style. Many people consider that the art of film-making would be set back 500 years, had Wagner not existed, with many film soundtracks owing their ability to enhance the story to Wagner alone. Almost all film composers, including John Williams, agree that Wagner is the greatest film composer in history; whole films can be set to his music.

Franz Schubert is said to be the greatest songwriter of all time, and one of the greatest masters of lyrical composition. Schubert possessed a natural mastery of all the forms of music, but loved songs the most, and wrote them so quickly that as soon as he was finished with one, it has been said that "he threw it to the floor and grabbed another sheet of paper to start another." He wrote "Hark, Hark, the lark," one of his finest, on the back of a beer hall receipt, in one sitting.(Quizlet, 2016)During Schubert's career of 16 years, he wrote approximately 650 songs.

His most famous work is his Piano Quintet, nicknamed the Trout, for the inclusion of one of his songs as a movement. He also wrote masses, 9 symphonies, of which the last two are universal brilliancies, sonatas, ballets, string quartets, and operas.(Quizlet, 2016) Schubert's finest works are his 8th and 9th symphonies, his Trout Quintet, ballet music to Rosamunde, Marche Militaire, and some of his songs, Gretchen, at the Spinning Wheel, The Erl-King, and Nacht und Träume among them.

Overall music started as a chant for rhythm and developed into a form of personality. It is a way for any person to think about messages or the meanings of life and capture them in a song. Being able to combine these words with the soothing rhythm of instruments is a talent that few are able to bring to the top.

Franz Schubert and Wolfgang Amadeus Mozart are only some of the many people that were able to see past the logic of the mind to create a form of art for many generations to listen to. They were able to look past the people around them who disliked the original symphonies and never saw them as high class people. These men were able to form a higher aspect for people to follow and a higher platform for future musicians to write upon.

In the different time periods and the different spaces of techniques through instruments, there are many ways to inspire people. There are many ways to motivate or find a positive message in history. Going through the facts allows for the opportunity to see something beyond yourself. Facts are able to give logic, and logic is able to give reason behind emotion. Some may argue that music has no use and that music is not able to give as much as artists wish to believe, but this is simply not true. Music is able to give more than the artists of history would ever be able to imagine. It is able to give a purpose to some and then a meaning to others. It is about how people will feel stuck, listen to a melody, and then be able to get back up. Seeing how the message of songs and a memorable rhythm can change the mind is truly a work of art inside of itself. It is about going through the day with a positive spirit rather than a dole perspective. If someone is having a bad day, then a single song coming from a symphony can change their entire day around.

Quiz:

Question 1: In what time period was the form of music called Opera invented?

Question 2: During the Romanticism Period, what were the compositions of poetic, visual, musical, and dramatic elements called? These compositions were created by Wilhelm Richard Wagner.

Question 3: Which German composer is known mainly to be one of the greatest composers of all time because of intellectual depth inside of the music, the artistic beauty of the music, and the technical command he had over the instruments?

Question 4: Who is known for writing seven of the longest operas ever known with four of them being the most famous masterpiece's in operas history?

Question 5: What is a short melody that is meant to represent a character, emotion, event, or object?

Chapter 3: The History of Jazz and Blues

In the times through the history of music itself, it is seen how people were enticed by the rhythm of chants and the sounds of soothing instruments. No matter what the music was about, the rhythm created a melody that people would be able to relax and focus upon the tales of life happening around them. In the more relaxing tones of music, comes the foundation of jazz and the blues. Here, music came as a comfort to the slaves working all day in the plantations in the 1800s. There were many people that attempted to go to church for the hymns and message found, but for the people who were not able to, there was this category.

The "Deep South" in the middle to the late 1800's was home to thousands of people who were slaves, ex-slaves and the descendants of slaves working in plantations and cotton fields of The Americas'. These mainly African-Americans sang as they toiled in the hot conditions as a form of relief and communication. "The blues" as a form of music originated with these people on these Southern plantations, from a mixture of African spirituals, chants, work songs, drum music, revivalist hymns, and country dance music. Unfortunately, much of this original music was not recorded and followed these musicians to their graves. But their legacy can still be heard in the 1920s and '30s recordings from Mississippi, Louisiana, Texas, Georgia and other Southern states.

Country blues music moved into the cities and spread, with many recognizable forms being created such as "St. Louis blues," "The Memphis Blues," "The Louisiana Blues," "The Mississippi Delta Blues," Chicago Blues," etc. Today there are many different variations of the blues, including Rhythm and Blues, Jump Blues, Boogie-Woogie, Swing, Barrelhouse and Ragtime as well as styles known as "The Cool Blues," a sophisticated piano-based form that owes much to jazz music. The Blues also found popularity in the United Kingdom with its own unique style from some well-known artists such as Peter Green, John Mayall, and Eric Clapton.

Jazz music grew out of the blues, during the 1898 war when the U.S. defeated Spain acquiring Puerto Rico and "liberating" Cuba. The troops that were coming back from the Caribbean front landed in New Orleans; they carried with them a multitude of assorted European brass instruments that had been used in the war marching bands. These instruments were surplus and so sold cheaply on the black market. Within a few years, the party city of New Orleans had a brass band in every neighborhood. The style in which these instruments were played was unique and heavily influenced by the different forms of blues and the syncopated rhythm of ragtime.

Because of racial discrimination and also because most "Black Musicians" were reluctant to record or share their music because of imitators, they were not often recorded until the 20's. Many people think Jazz originated from African American's, which is certainly true of the blues. But Jazz or "syncopated orchestra" as it was called until the mid-20's, mainly because of the instruments used, was as multiracial music of the new Americans incorporating strong blues influences as well as European. The term Dixieland Jazz was the commercialization of the style; it was mainly recorded by white artists to sell to white audiences and often really just mimicked some styles of black music.

One of the most Famous Jazz artists was a trumpet player Louis "Satchmo" Armstrong, who was a charming and flamboyant player who knew how to entertain an audience. He became famous for his improvisations on covers of blues and pop standards which influenced generations of jazz musicians and fans, but his jazz became more style than substance, although his influence was enormous and his style made jazz a worldwide phenomenon.

This artist created a masterpiece to beyond even today. Looking back on how history was created and how he was able to entertain the people around him, he created a high standard for people to follow. When someone hears a trumpet player or a piano player and thinks about how they compare to others, they go through to the past, but not too far back. In the times of discrimination, there was more to be seen towards the perspective of the slaves and African Americans. While they moved through the plantations to create a certain part of the economy, they were still people who later on had a burden of the past they were forced to carry through their lives.

Traditions of the past and the rhythm of music all have the same timeline to follow. As they go through history to find the right place to start, people are able to find how people change and how people go through periods with different thoughts. While it is true that the rhythm of some matched the rhythm of others, it is a mistake that is attempted to not be repeated in the future. The past will remain in the past, but it is important to see the past in order to provide a greater future. This same idea is mainly said for times of battle and war, but music fits in another category on its own. No matter who created the rhythm or who created the lyrics, it always was able to serve the same kind of purpose to people.

Music has always been able to change the days or even change the life of people in general. It is a way to step away from the views of reality and step into the thoughts of the mind. It is a beauty that all people are able to share. While some people like jazz and other people like rap and other people like pop, all of these share the same beginning. All of these things share the same results. People are happier when listening to the instruments and the calm rhythm of music, and it is all thanks to the people of the past to create the joy of the modern day through music.

Quiz:

Question 1: "The blues" is a form of music that originated from where?

Question 2: Jazz grew from the music called "the blues". During the war is 1898 where the U.S. defeated Spain, where did the troops land to sell their European brass instruments?

Chapter 4: The History of Rock Music

In the lyrics of one of Buddy Guy's famous songs are "The Blues had a baby, and they called it rock n' roll," which explains the transformation of many of the artists of the day into rock stars. The late 1940s and early 1950s saw the birth of Rock n' Roll from a combination of styles including blues, boogie-woogie, jump blues, jazz, gospel, western swing and country music. It was popular with teenagers in America and Europe with artists performing live in most areas. Early forms often used the piano or saxophone as the lead instrument with later styles, adding drums, a double bass, and electric guitars.

Rock n' Roll was much more than simply a musical style;it took the world by storm with huge concerts and packed dance halls worldwide, the advent of television brought it into people's living rooms and radio stations played it nonstop.

Rock n' Roll was also seen in movies, it had such an influence on young people's lifestyles, fashion, attitudes, and language, that it had parents and public figures up in arms trying to have it banned. Rock n' Roll by the 1960's had evolved into what is now called "Rock Music" or "Rock," with different variations such as Punk Rock, Electric Rock, Metal and Heavy Metal, Rock a Billy, New Age, etc.

The Beatles

The Beatles were a Rock and Pop band formed in Liverpool in 1960. The band members John Lennon, Paul McCartney, George Harrison and Ringo Star are widely regarded as the foremost and most influential band ever, a band by which nearly everything else in pop music is matched and measured. Their influence on artists that followed their phenomenal single decade career from 1960 to 1970 is immeasurable.

The Beatles built their reputation playing clubs in Liverpool, London, and Hamburg, Germany, over a three-year period from 1960. Their Manager Brian Epstein molded them into a professional act, and their producer George Martin guided and developed their recordings, greatly expanding their popularity in the United Kingdom. "Beatlemania" spread widely in Britain and by early 1964 The Beatles had become international superstars, leading the "British Invasion" of the United States pop market and the rest of the world.

The Beatles are the best-selling music artists in the U.S. with 178 million certified units sold; they have had more number-one albums on the British charts and sold more singles in the UK than any other act. They are the world's best-selling band, with estimated sales of over 600 million records worldwide. All members of the "Fab four" The Beatles group were inducted into the Rock n' Roll Hall of Fame individually as well as in the band. After the band's breakup in 1970, they each enjoyed successful musical careers of varying lengths. McCartney and Starr, the 2 surviving members, remain musically active today. Lennon was shot and killed in December 1980, and Harrison died of lung cancer in November 2001.

The Stones

The Rolling Stones - another English rock band formed in London in 1962, they along with the Beatles were extremely popular in all areas of the world. The Rolling Stones were perceived by the youth of Britain and then the world as representatives of the opposition to the old world order and authoritarian culture. They were instrumental in making blues a major part of rock and roll and of changing the international focus of blues. Robert Palmer, a musicologist, attributed the "remarkable endurance" of the Rolling Stones to being "rooted in traditional varieties, in rhythm-and-blues and soul music." The Rolling Stones have continued to be a huge attraction on the live circuit, with big stadium tours in the 1990s and 2000s. By 2007, the band had made what were then four of the top five highest-grossing concert tours of all time.

The "Stones" have estimated album sales of over 250 million; they have released twenty-nine studio albums, eighteen live albums, and numerous compilations. In 2012, the band celebrated its 50th anniversary and is still going strong today.

Elvis

Elvis Aaron Presley (1935 to 1977) was an American musician and actor who is often referred to as the "King"; he was regarded as one of the most significant cultural icons of the 20th century. Presley was born in Mississippi and moved to Memphis, Tennessee when he was 13 years old. His music recording career began there in 1954. Presley's first RCA single, "Heartbreak Hotel" was released in January 1956 and became a number-one hit in the United States. After a series of successful network television appearances and chart-topping records, he was soon regarded as the leading figure of rock'n'roll, with his energized interpretations of songs and sexually provocative performance style, combined with a singularly potent mix of influences across color lines made him enormously popular and controversial.

In November 1956, he made his film debut and in 1958, he was drafted into military service for 2 years. After which he resumed his recording career, producing some of his most commercially successful work before devoting much of the 1960s to making Hollywood films and their accompanying soundtrack albums. In 1968, he returned to the stage in the acclaimed televised comeback special "Elvis" which led to many concerts and a string of highly profitable tours. In 1973, Presley was featured in the first globally broadcast concert via satellite, "Aloha-from Hawaii," Several years of prescription drug abuse severely damaged his health, and he died in 1977 at the age of 42.

Presley is one of the most celebrated and influential musicians of the 20th century, he is the bestselling solo artist in the history of the world, with estimated record sales of around 600 million units worldwide. He won three Grammy awards and the Grammy Lifetime Achievement Award as well as being inducted into a variety of music halls of fame.

Bill Haley

William John Clifton(Bill) Haley (1925 to 1981) was credited as one of the first American rock n' roll musicians, with his group Bill Haley and His Comets they popularized rock n' roll in the early 1950's, selling over 25 million records worldwide. Their titles include; "Rock around the Clock," "See You Later Alligator," Rocket 88," "Skinny Minnie," and Razzle Dazzle," with "Shake Rattle and Roll" becoming the first ever rock n' roll song to enter the British singles charts in December 1954, becoming a Gold Record. Haley and his band played an important part in launching Rock n' Roll to a wider audience after a period of it being considered an underground genre.

Quiz:

Question 1: Who was the musician who had a major influence on many people of different races?

Chapter 5: Country and Western Music

Country or country and western music originated from the folk songs, ballads and popular songs of the English, Scottish and Irish settlers in the U.S. It is mainly written and performed by white Americans depicting emotions and experiences of poor white people, telling their stories of illicit love, passion, crime, and prison life. Western music tends to have a flavor of ranching and cowboys and the old west. Country music tends to be simpler and more similar to folk music; it uses fewer instruments, relying on guitar, fiddle, banjo, and harmonica.

Western music, by contrast, often uses more electronic instruments and big band sounds, it first became popular from cowboy movies and western music, an often heard expression from "Country and Western" fans is for someone to say "There are only two types of music; Country and Western, and I like both of them." These two styles began to mix together in the 1920's, at this time there were many new recording companies who were promoting and recording all types of music in rural areas. During World War II, when different sections of Americans met and mixed together, the outcome was a variety of new variations of many traditional styles of country music, which also branched out and mixed with blues music to form rock n' roll.

Quiz:

Question 1: Country and Western Music was created to depict the experiences and emotions of who?

Question 2: Country music branched out and mixed together with blues music in order to create what type of music?

Chapter 6: Electronic Music

Electronic music became possible with the development of recording technology, which made all types of sounds available for potential use as musical material. The term "Electronic Music" usually refers to a repertory of art, music developed in the 1950s in Europe, Japan, and the Americas. By using magnetic tape, composers could record a variety of sounds and then arrange them in a musical way. Electronic music depends on transmission via loudspeakers, but there are two broad types, those that exist only in recorded form known as acousmatic music and live electronic music, in which electronic apparatus is used to generate, transform, or trigger sounds during a performance by musicians using voices, traditional instruments, electro-acoustic instruments, or other devices. Starting in 1957, the use of computers became increasingly important to record, mix and store this form of music. Music or the material used to make music was gathered or acoustical sounds of the everyday world, the term to describe it was "musique concrete" when the sound the sounds were produced by electronic generators, it was "designated electronic music," but after the 1950's, the term "electronic music" came to be used for both types.

Often electronic music was combined with more conventional instruments in the late 1950's and 60's; many bands started to use it including "The Beach Boys" and "The Beatles." By the end of the 60's the only bands that did not use electronic music were some Traditional Blues and Folk bands. With the invention of the Moog synthesizer, many new progressive rock bands such as "Pink Floyd," "Yes," "Emerson, Lake and Palmer," "Genesis," and Brian Eno of "Roxy Music" made electronic music part of their sounds.

Japanese electronic rock was produced by several musicians, including Isao Tomita's "Electric Samurai – Switched on Rock" and Osamu kitajima's album "Benzaiten", both featuring Moog synthesizers and European artists like Jean Michel Jarre, Vangelis and Brian Eno, who all influenced the upcoming "new age music" and "Punk Rock" which led to a

[26]

new form of basic electronic rock that was relying on new digital technology to replace other instruments. Pioneering bands for this new electronic music included "Ultravox," "Yellow Magic Orchestra," "Gary Numan and "The Human League," with the development of digital audio made it much easier to produce purely electronic sounds which led to the growth of "synthpop," the use of which started to dominate the pop and rock music of the early 80s.Bands like Duran Duran," "Spandau Ballet," "A Flock of Seagulls," "Culture Club," "Talk Talk," and "The Eurythmics" often used synthesizers to replace all other instruments, until the style began to fall from popularity in the mid-1980s.

Quiz:

Question 1: What is the term used to describe the music created and gathered by acoustical sounds of the everyday world?

Question 2: What is the term used to describe the music created by electronic generators?

Chapter 7: Pop Music

Abba was the bestselling 'Pop' group in the world from 1974 until about 1982, although they were not so popular in the US, they were international superstars and a lot of people consider their highly melodic, catchy songs to be the gold standard in pop music. In more recent years they have enjoyed a bit of a comeback due to the musical "Mamma Mia" that is based around their songs.

Michael Jackson

Michael Jackson's album "Thriller" was the best-selling album of all time, and he was the world's biggest pop star, with the possible exception of Elvis. Jackson started his career as a child of 11 in 1969 with his brothers in the group Jackson 5 before pursuing a solo career weathering tabloid rumors and criminal investigations, but he was ever popular until his death at the age 50 in 2009.

Elton John

Elton John's singing and piano playing make him one of the top in pop music history. He has released over 50 top 40 singles, including an amazing 38 consecutive top 40 singles from 1972 to 1986. His music is considered definitive of mainstream pop in the 1970s; recently he has frequently toured with fellow successful piano playing pop musician, Billy Joel.

Quiz:

Question 1: What album did Michael Jackson create that was the best-selling album of all time?

Question 2: What was Elton John known for that made him one of the top musicians in pop music history?

Chapter 8: Prehistoric Music and Instruments

When looking at different time periods from around the world, there are a multitude of cultures that comes together to create a certain personality for every part of land. The history of music in Ireland will be different from the history of music in Europe or Britain. In this section of prehistoric music, it is all about the overall sections of music. This is where everyone on the planet lived together as one unit. People would hunt and gather materials only for the sense of survival. Once people started to figure out different ways of hunting and gathering, this was when different cultures started to develop. Even though it is only a small seed of culture, this is where it began.

With the seed that began music, prehistoric instruments mainly came from bone. After people hunted, they looked and attempted to use every part of the animals they hunted. The oldest type of instrument that was found is called the bone flute. This kind of flute was found deep with the caves of France and Germany. When researchers looked to investigate the musical instrument to see how people developed them, they were able to find cave art that was around 37,000 to 40,000 years old. The art is as old as the instrument.

Once people began to create their own sense of music in the caves, a cultural impact began to develop. In these prehistoric and ancient times, people would look to gods and believe that their high influence began the invention of the sounds echoing from the instruments from the walls of the cave. With this influence came the impact of battle and war from the Persians. The Persians create an instrument called a mouth pipe that was used during the Celtic war. These were used to communicate with the people on their side and stimulate the hope within them as the pipe was able to terrify the enemy. From here, people were able to see that music is able to create a feeling of spiritual awareness as it is able to induce fear and joy within any person.

Stone Age: During the time of the Stone Age, the bone flute was created in the caves where people lived and gathered their supplies. With the appearance of the bone flute came the introduction of some of the first rock art. Experiments and researchers have been able to shown a connection between the images in the caves and the acoustic properties of the wall. In a cave with how the walls are shaped, there are parts that will let out different sounds. Researchers believe that the walls chosen for the cave art were the same places that people mainly played their instruments. When people in prehistoric times has a ritual inside of the cave, they would draw or paint on the walls as another person would play the bone flute. It was a way to go through their life to show appreciation and entertain towards each other.

There were many types of bones that were used for flutes and whistles with the most common types of bones being the leg or wing bones found in different birds. The oldest kind of bone flute that was found was in Germany, and it was made from the radius of a hooper swan. Other times, there were other animal bones or even human bones that were used for the flute.

After bone was found to be used as a musical instrument, stone was used in order to imitate bird and animal sounds. A stone flute is able to create a type of whistle that is able to call in birds closer for hunting. To make these stone flutes, a stone was bored through by a shellfish that is able to drill holes into the stone before it is washed up on the beach. People would search careful for the right stone that had the right kind of sound to use for hunting.

Stones were also used in the rather simple way of simply clicking two stones together to create a rhythm or beat. The size and shape of the stone was able to have a different stone come out. The harder a person clicked the two stones together, the sharper the sound was. There were other large rocks that were able to create a certain ringing sound when they were struck. These ringing sounds were used repeatedly during times of rituals as people would also look to find flat stones that could be lined together on the ground. Once they were lined together, a person would be able to take a stick and strike the stones. It was a difficult sound, but in the right hands it was seen to be the highest for rhythm and sharpness of sound.

The bow and arrow are known mainly to be a weapon, but during the Stone Age it was also used as a musical instrument. When the string was put on a string with enough tension to cause the stick to bend into a shape of a bow, it also was able to make a sound. A light tap on the string would be able to create a small sound that could be amplified by attaching a hollow vessel at one of the end or by the mouth cavity of the player.

The first instrument that was a lip read is actually from an animal horn. These animal horns are normally from cattle, sheep, goats, or even antelope. These horns were easily accessible as they are easy to play and even easier to create. The horn of a ram was actually blessed and carved by a rabbi to become a shofar; an important part of the Jewish faith. This instrument was able to be used in marriage or celebrations of the family. They were a way to go through and spread the sounds of joy within people. The horn was able to have a louder sound that could be echoed throughout the land. The flowing curve and the shape of the cattle horn became rather popular as they were a kind of reward. Having the courage to hunt a larger animal and having a prize to have people across many distances to hear.

The last kind of instrument during the Stone Age was called the 'Bodhran'. This was a type of simple frame drum. It had a narrow hoop of wood that was surrounded by animal skin stretched all the way across it and secured to one side. These kind of frame drums were very common during the prehistoric times and even during the present day. This instrument with a stick was able to have a complex rhythm to allow a tune to be shared with the other instruments.

Early Bronze Age: In the Early Bronze Age, it all began with the discovery of the wooden tube or wooden pipes. These were a type of wind instrument that are still used today. The instrument was a combination of many pipes tied together. Imagine taking a dozen so wooden pipes laid out together on the floor. Tie them together or glue them together and be sure that they are all still laid flat. The different sounds in this instrument comes from the length of each of the pipes. The first wooden tube can even be a third of the size of the last wooden tube attached to the instrument. Some people would create larger instruments that were made up of thirty or so wooden pipes. During this time, people would go through and investigate how the pipe could sound with different lengths and different sharpness of breadth coming from the player.

Time went on into the Middle to Late Bronze Age where the horns from the sheep and cattle from the Stone Age actually started to develop into bronze horns. The bronze horn is known to be one of the largest collections of instruments from prehistoric times as it is well known to the plains of Ireland. These bronze horns were made to be in a variety of different shapes and sizes depending on the use of the instrument. Some of the more artistic shaped bronze horn instruments were used for weddings while the bigger instruments were used for spiritual practices.

The next instrument that developed during this time was called the Crotal. This instrument is best described to be a kind of rattle or bell. It was able to fit well in the hand as the instrument was about the size of an avocado. They were a hollow cast of bronze that was filled with a single stone or pebble. When the instrument was shaken, it would cause a rapid rattle and allow for a high pitched ringing. Because of the value of the bronze and the higher level of welding and casting of the instrument, it was seen to be very expensive. Since they were at a high value, not many people used them or had them at all. They were used strictly for rituals for the gods to appeal to their kindness in the hopes for better land and better seasons for crops.

Iron Age: In the time of the Iron Age, the highest instrument known was called the Loughnashade Trumpa. The best way to think about this kind of instrument is as a long trumpet. In prehistoric times, the bronze horn was thinned out to be about two meters long with a thickness of about .5mm. Since the main body of the instrument is a small diameter, it is very light. It weighed less than 1 kilo as people were then able to use it easily for transportation and they were able to use it for celebrations that happened farther away. They rose in popularity with a design plate placed around the top of the thin tube. The design plate had no effect on the sound, but it allowed for the personality of the player to be seen. The creator of the instrument would be able to have different curves and symbols on this plate as they were able to go through and customize it.

This instrument was played as a curved shape with the top of the instrument high in the air. Other instruments were shaped in the way of an 'S'. The design plate was always facing forward with the top of the design plate high in the air each time. They were always played in a rather sweet E flat harmonic size series. The pressure and shockwave of the breadth inside of the small thin tube created the powerful sound that was able to blast out of the instrument. The powerful sound would be used in battle to move the troops forward. Not only was that, but the shockwave that was able to go through the instrument continued to be able to help the troops get into the action of battle. It is the same way that songs used today that have an upbeat sound or rhythm are able to motivate people. They are able to go through and get people to stand up and see how much they are able to do in life.

On the other side though, there was an instrument that let out a more delicate and sweet sound when compared to the trumpas. This instrument was called the Ard Brinn, and it was made out of two parts. Two tubes with one being cylindrical and the second tube was longer. When they were joined together, they created a shallow 'S' curve that came out overall to be 239.5 cm in length. The fitting that allowed the two tubes to join together was made out of a brass connector. The instrument was played many times and it was able to play about a dozen notes. It mainly played a B fundamental over many years through the times of celebration and rejoice.

Early Medieval Instruments: In these times, the first instrument that was discovered was called the River Erne. It was a wooden horn that was attached together with multiple metal bindings. It came out all together to be about 58 cm long. With a metal mouth piece attached to one end, people would be able to have more control of the pitch of each sound that came out as they would begin using this instrument in different forms of art. It was of such great importance that a painting was created of two of these instruments being played during the 8th century AD.

Overall, there are many types of music that were created during the prehistoric times. Whether the instrument came from bone or from metal, each instrument was meant for the purpose of celebration and art. When a person found or created their own instrument, they were adding a part of culture to their own tribe. Since people would go through to hunt down animals and gather the necessary supplies of survival, they would have no time for truly sitting down and exploring the pitch of instruments. The moment that someone would walk in with a bone flute, they were able to see how the tribe could manage their time and be able to have an exploration of rituals.

It never began as playing instruments for the sound. Instead, it was about playing the instrument to find a sense of communication and hope. Whenever they played an instrument, they were hoping to talk to the gods in the faith for a better farming season or more cattle. They would go through and see how the pitch of the instrument could be heard far and wide, so people would use it in battle. Calling out to all the troops to march forward and see what they are fighting for. Either way, these simple instruments were able to create the different ideas of sound through pipes as they were able to set a foundation for the kind of music that is known to people today.

Quiz:

Question 1: What was the first kind of instrument found to be created?

Question 2: During what time period was the use of metal with instruments started?

Question 3: What was the main purpose of having the musical instrument in prehistoric times?

Chapter 9: Love of Music Explained

When people are listening to a song, there is always an emotion or thought that is attached to it. It is simply a situation that people experience without any form of practice or special ability. Being able to love music is something that everyone has in common. People are able to go through the lyrics of a song, the beat of the instruments, and they instantly are away from the world, but people wonder why this really happens.

In daily life, people go through needing to talk through their job or present themselves to another person. When they do not know what to say or if they simply are just preparing for a speech, listening to a song can inspire the words chosen. Music is able to come into the thoughts of a person to give the words that could not have been thought of at first. It is about stating how you are feeling and telling someone how you truly feel. Doing this can be difficult, but a song can provide the answers that were not seen before. The other way to see this is how music will be an escape from everyday life. It will be able to provide another world to escape to or another imagination to develop. There is something about listening to music that takes people away from the moment. It is as if they are listening to people, but they are fulling concentrated on the people. The same idea goes for music. People will put headphones on, and suddenly the world around them will disappear. No matter if you are driving to work or on the bus to school, music will pass the time and help to relax you on the way there.

One of the best ways to think about music is how it connects people together. People of different cultures and backgrounds are able to come together since they enjoy the same song or the same style of music. A single song is able to bind people through diversity. Even if the song is in a different language, people may enjoy the rhythm. Then suddenly people who do not even speak the same language are going through emotional songs together. Just because the lyrics cannot be heard does not mean that the song cannot be moving to people.

After finding the right words to say and having the escape from the real world, music is still used to help people show an understanding to their loved ones. A song is able to show how someone is feeling. If someone normally listens to hard rock when they are happy but jazz when they are sad, then people would be able to see when that person is upset. Having your own personal taste in music is able to give a personality to yourself as it is able to go through and create a baseline for people to start a conversation. But if no one is really there to realize that you are upset, then music by itself is able to be there to relax and calm you down. A music list can be an instant mood lifter as it is able to be an escape and an answer. Even if someone is simply trying to pass the time and get through the day, music can fill in and be the entertainment.

Since music is able to be an instant mood lifter and then it is able to bring people together, music is able to create memories. Listening to a song helps a person to remember things that happened in the past. It is able to connect people together for new experiences. One of the best things music is for is road trips and movies. On the long road, music helps people to see the world around them as they are then able to enjoy each other instead of being bored. In the movies, music is used to get people to watch the movie again and again. People will remember the scenes that have a song and a cool rhythm. When they leave the movie and hear that song later on, they instantly remember the scene they heard the song from. This helps not only for the advertising of the movie, but it helps for people to go back and remember a joyful memory.

But the true curiosity here is how the mind is able to get all of this from a simple song. Yes, songs can be deep and powerful in the lyrics, but this is a lot to get from a combination of instruments. Being able to look past the real world for a certain period of time is a concept that is hard to imagine only one thing solving. Being able to find the right words to describe a feeling is another hard thing to imagine only one thing solving. It is the idea that there are many different things that exist in this world, but music it a precious gem that everyone can use to connect and find answers for.

The Science behind music goes through to see how the mind takes in the rhythm and how the thoughts then interpret them to help with the stability of emotions. The beat and melody of the song is able to trigger both feelings and emotions inside of people. It is able to create joy, sadness, and a sense of wonder. Not only that, but it is able to bring back treasured memories back from childhood. But how is it able to go through and do everything listed above? How is the list possible just from a simple form of sound? In reality, hunting is needed for survival so it would make sense to have that activity at the top, but instead music is ranked higher.

Scientists have looked into the possibility for the reasons why this is all happening, they were able to conclude that music triggers activity in the nucleus accumbens. This is the same brain structure that is able to release the chemical dopamine that gives out the sensation of pleasure. When someone is eating and they simply get happy by the taste, which is because of the chemical. The same story goes for music; listening to a song releases some of the chemical as it is then able to give joy to the person.

The nucleus accumbens is only a part of the whole process though. It turns out that music will also activate the amygdala. The amygdala is involved in the process of emotion and the prefrontal cortex for abstract decision making. When going through the day and deciding to turn on the radio to pass the time or to think about life, that is the part of the prefrontal cortex. That decision made will be able to give the mind something to look forward to as the chemical dopamine will release soon after.

Quiz:

Question 1: (True or False) Music helps to connect people of different cultures and helps for people to find answers or find themselves in life.

Question 2: What is the chemical released while listening to music?

Chapter 10: Music in Modern Society

Music is able to do wonders for each and every person. It is able to tie people together of different cultures and languages, and yet it is still able to bring a smile to any individual person. Every decade or era of time is paired with a certain style of music. There is music from the 80's, then music from the 90's, and then music from the 60's. Music is a kind of imprint into cultural reality as it is able to create such a powerful feeling to people. But outside of what it does for people, it is able to have an even larger impact on society.

Look at a single decade and look at the music that defined it. Saying the phrase 'defined it' is the main key phrase here. Each time of music is carved out by what the decade was about. The ideas that people believed in and the trends that existed are all found in the lyrics and melody of the music in that decade. Another way to think of it is how music is a narrator. It is able to say what people have gone through and what people are growing to become. Here, people believe that without music, people would not be able to live as long. This is because of the idea that music is able to suppress emotions so well that without it people would slowly destroy themselves through all the stress and tensions found in life. It is a form of art that is able to define both people and their events of the time.

When wars happen or the economy is struggling, the personal emotions of the musicians feeling the effects of the war and the economy come out through the song. It is not only the musician that feels the pain, but everyone feels the pain. Even though people realize this truth, there is something about listening to a song and realizing that you are not alone in the pain that you are feeling at the moment. Knowing that the people around you are feeling the same thing is a connection in society that creates a bond of hope. The second part that musicians do is create their own hope or motivation in a song. Letting people know that times are rough, but there is light found in every shadow. This allows for people to calm down a little bit more as they are able to see that there is a chance in the world. They are able to see that things will turn better. In times of sorrow, it is easy to look away and stay that things will remain terrible no matter what. The moment a song comes on to show that the pain is real but the hope is real too, people see that the bad situation is not the end of everything.

Going back to each and every part of life where people felt stuck, they always felt alone and scared. But everyone has the same ability to listen to the song. Everyone is able to go through and have their own playlist. The fact that every person can do this is a large impact on society. It allows for everyone to express themselves to one another. They are then able to have another sense of culture to be able to show.

Cultural Impact of popular music shows what people are going through during their own daily lives. The fingerprints and life of each and every generation can be found within the lyrics of songs. The rhythm of the songs show how every footstep was taken during that decade. This can be seen as individual or as a whole. For the purposes of society, the footsteps taken were more about political power and the ability to go through together as one group to get through the troubles of the decade. Everyone has a purpose in standing together, and music guides people to see what they need to do. If they are lost, then music can show how they were able to create the culture in the first place.

Culture and music are able to flow together to create a kind of power to grow within people. It is able to being appealing to the people of that generation or the people of that decade to use later on. It is how music is able to recreate the thoughts of memories inside of a person. For example, a parent may enjoy the music from the 80's more than modern music since the music from the 80's would bring more thoughts towards their own memories. It is also the music they were built upon and the music that carved the culture that created who they are today. A child would listen to the same music and may not enjoy it as much since the music they enjoy is more modern.

The more modern music draws in the culture that the child has developed with. It is not about how music becomes outdated, but it is more about how the music reflects how the person became who they are.

The Moral Impact of music on society is easiest to see on an individual level rather than together with society. To begin, think about beliefs and thoughts together. How a belief is able to grow into a behavior. Then how a behavior is able to grow a personality in a person. At the start, a belief is simply what a child hears or wishes to believe. Whether it is from parents or from a show, a belief is simply a belief. As the child grows older and begins thinking on their own, they begin to choose what to believe and they begin to choose their own ways. When people go through to have a belief, they then choose it through an inspiration, this is where music comes in.

Music is able to sell itself as well as a message. Listening to rap music encourages a rush inside of people. Listening to pop music encourages a motivation inside of a person. No matter how people look at music, it is still able to speak for itself. There are still arguments on what different types of music say. No matter what people say the music is supposed to say or what the music is blamed to show, it still shows something. People will listen to the music when they are lost. The song is able to guide them to what they should be. When someone is preparing for a test but they do not feel the motivation or the speed to prepare for the test. A fast paced song or a song explaining the pain of hope or explaining the faith in future can allow for the person to go through and get ready for the test.

Morals and behaviors are strongly persuaded when people are growing to become adults. Mainly in their teen years the lyrics of a song can mean everything. They can go through the rage of seeing that no one else is able to understand them as much as a song does. While a song is not necessarily the main point of the behavior, it continues to have a rather strong influence over people. Since this does happen, it is important to be careful about the interactions a person has and the words that they listen to. It is not good to have a sad person listen to a song that provokes death. The same idea goes for how people that are getting ready for a big celebration should be careful on how many upbeat songs they listen too. No matter what people say a song should be, there should still be a certain amount of care that goes into the amount of songs a person listens too. Either way, this subject continues to be explored or there are many parts to the idea of behavior. Even though music is a part of it, which does not mean that it cannot be a bad thing to people. It is about knowing the right step to take forward.

The Emotional Impact can be seen through how a person feels when they listen to a song. They are able to feel like more than themselves. They are able to see past the pain and look more into the future. As a society, people have to go together to see how much can be done. Stepping forward together to allow for a certain atmosphere to develop. Music is able to create the atmosphere and it is able to create the first step for people to follow. It is about how people will listen to upbeat music when they are working out, or they listen to jazz on a romantic date, or they will dance when they hear pop music with a good beat. All of these things create an atmosphere for people to follow. It is an atmosphere to bring people together.

The Political Impact of music is a subject that is difficult to begin. Since there are many different views on how people view politics and how people argue on the subject, it is able to go through many loops. With people on one side going completely against the beliefs of people on the other side, it is difficult to see how music would be able to cure or even bring up any kind of foundation for this problem.

While issues occur in the arguments, the connection between politics and music has existed in many cultures. The art of a song has been able to allow for many influences in political movements and other forms of rituals. Music is able to create an establishment for protests while it is also able to create reasons to go against protests. It is able to create both a positive feature and a negative feature in the minds of people. This thought can get rather confusing, and the best way to make it clear is to think about a country's national anthem. The national anthem is a song, no matter where it exists in the world. It is able to bring people together, bring support to those losing hope, bring motivation to soldiers, and bring a reason to fight or defend. On the other side, the national anthem to another person's eyes can be a signal for controversy or attack if they do not agree with the ways of the land that the national anthem is a part of. This is all about perspective, and having a single song state the perspective of an entire national allows for support and at the same time it allows for others to see a place worthy to take over. No matter what lyrics or song is played, opposite sides will always occur in the world.

The next way to think about the connection between music and politics is through a political campaign. Being able to create a slogan that has a certain 'ring' to it creates both a bond and a memorable statement for people to remember when voting. In order to have the most votes out of all the candidates, it is best to think about the ways that allows for the person to stand out the most. Once this happens, then conversations begin to rise and people begin seeing a reason to continue through the process of researching the candidate. Having a memorable rhythm in the political campaign allows for the thought of that specific candidate to stick in the mind of the person. They then are able to go to the voting booths remembering the reasons why they chose this person. All of this was able to start through the idea of having a memorable part of the campaign.

Not only can music portray a reason to remember a candidate during a political campaign, but it is also able to allow for a specific political message. It is able to tie together the references of history and the events that inspired the present events. It is about how they are able to look farther ahead than the other candidates and give the people an answer in the format that is pleasing to the ear. When a candidate decides to sell a message through a speech, it is better to go through the words in the same way that people would want. This is not to stay that political candidates should start having rap battles to see who is the best. Instead, it is about presentation. Being able to show yourself as more than lines on a sheet of paper.

Since there are many ways for music to be seen as political in a sense, there are some forms of music that have already been called political only by simple cultural association and other forms of irrespective political content. For example, The Beatles were a Western pop and rock band that became censored by the state in the 1960s and 1970s since they were seen to be a symbol of social change to the younger people. Since the band caused a reaction inside of people and caused them to begin asking more than answering, the state saw a reason to go in and do something about it. With the music being able to cause such a large and wild change, it is able to continue in forming different looks of controversy with people.

Looking at how the idea of political music would be able to sound, it is difficult to go through and simply take it in as a good head start. It is about how the political music does make people wonder. It is about how in this form of music, there is a moment of actions farther than a message. Normal songs will tell people to stay strong while a political song will take this same message one step forward. With how soft this one detail can become, it is difficult for these songs to completely stand out. They are difficult to go through in front of an audience and they are even harder to go through with in having to find funding.

Quiz:

Question 1: What are the main types of impacts that music has on society?

Question 2: In the political aspect, why was it difficult to play music in front of an audience?

Chapter 11: Folk Music in Europe, Asia, Africa, and South America

Folk music is a type of music that is found from an origin of culture. It is difficult to define, but the best way to see it is as a kind of music done by composers who are not known. The melody created was used for dances and tales and a traditional ritual. The melody would then be passed down to many people over the generations to come in order to spread an influence of culture.

Folk music overall came from England through the people who told stories and were able to continue through the times of trouble to find a legend through the art of music. It is overall seen to be an expression of life that has developed in multiple ways around people in general. It was mainly through the 30s and 40s that folk music was able to have a rise in popularity as it continued through a time where artists like Jimmy Rogers created a style of music with a sense of honour and a reproduction of the folk music from the past. No matter what was needed to get through the ways to replicate the music, it was still found in multiple places throughout the world.

Around the world, there are different tales and legends that are told, and at the same time there are different instruments that are chosen for folk music. Moving from the idea of one country to another, people had different resources to use, and they did their best to have the music they wanted to hear during their traditional celebrations and rituals.

In Europe, folk music is a difficult subject to go through since there is very little material on where it came from or how the existence of it was able to have an impact. There is not much evidence found today to prove that each song had a certain age to it. When going through the idea of fold music, each song should be able to have an estimated date or timeline with it in order to find the composer of the song. Instead, in Europe, little evidence was gather or found to create a list of the folk music within their continent.

The largest part to consider with folk music is the mutual contact with people. Villagers with their instruments would be able to travel from the court to village with their songs being played for all to hear. This was one of the first times where people would be able to hear a melody of music outside of rituals, celebrations, and churches. Performers would then be able to hear each other's music and compare. They were not looking to compete, but instead they were looking to improve. Seeing how they could add to their own music and add to their own style. The contact between the types of musical styles between people increased by itself once the invention of printing came about in the fifteenth century. This was large in the areas of Western Europe. The aspect of printing was able to give a good method of dissemination to allow for a close relationship between the music of the song and the people of the villages.

The most well-known part of the European Folk Music is called the Strophic Form. This was a type of line structure that the folk music was able to be created upon. It is a type of tune that repeats several lines over and over again. It was able to create great length in a song and it was able to have Europe stand out since other areas of folk music did not carry out with this kind of tradition. Some appear in the North American Indian cultures, far over in the regions of Africa, Asia, and in the Middle East. Overall, it is the basic principle that either the tune or the portion of the tune can be sung more than once. It could be sung with different words, but the melody of the notes would repeat.

Since this was a unique characteristic of folk music in Europe, it was then able to carry through to create the same idea with poetry. It is the idea of folk poetry in which the writer of the poem could repeat the lines of the poem in units of two, three, or even six lines. The lines repeated were not a part of the number of syllable or the poetic feet. Instead it was more so interrelated through the aspect of a rhyme scheme. Being able to leave the poem with a different structure each time as the flow of the poem would be able to repeat. It is the transition from a repeated poetic structure to a repeated melody.

In Asia the folk music carries on to be about how the music ties together the style of the music, the dancing, and the instruments. It is still difficult to find the areas of information in this country since music scholars have a difficult time connecting the ideas of the melody with the history of the subject. Asian music history though does go on to provide a multiplicity of instruments as well as a wide range of information for the performing arts. It is where the culture was created as the composers of the folk music would go through to use flutes, fiddles, and drums for the folk music.

The most common flutes discovers were called the Sybyzgy, Choor, Tar, Tanbur, and the Rawap. The most common fiddles found were the Kyrgyz and the Ghijak. The most common drums found were the basic kettle drum, the frame drum, and the Dayra. The last instrument most commonly found was the harp along with other string type instrument known mainly to be Rubab, Dutar, and Bombra. Since there is a wide assortment of names for the instruments, it is able to show how folk music was able to impact their society. Each instrument had a voice, and playing them in union created a fair melody for the people to hear. For the string instruments, researchers believe that the namads actually used snake skin and horse hair to create them. The other types of instruments were created from bamboo. These kind of techniques are able to be traced back all the way to the times of the Qin dynasty, Tang dynasty, and the Han dynasty. In Ancient China, the kings and rulers would send out officials to listen into the songs traveling around the villages. They would see what was the most popular and then they would bring it back for entertainment.

Southern Asia had a wide assortment of folk music to define the history that it had. This included both the classic and the popular types of folk music. While the music does stand on its own with the bamboo type of instruments, there was still a historical connection to Indian culture. The traditional type of Indian culture was able to surround the ideas of Hindustani and Carnatic music. Purandara Dasa was the founder of Carnatic music to cover all the areas of the popular folk music.

The culture itself of West Asia and South East Asia is completely different with the ways of music history. The people in West Asia were able to invent the ghazals which was a mixture of both European and Latin America styles. From there, they connected in history to create the form of music called Pakistan. This type of music is rather diverse in the ways of population and brand of music. Simply think of it as the ways rock n' roll is found in modern society. It has its own footprint and popularity, but not much comparison besides how it was able to originate from other genres. Pakistani music ranges all over South Asia to create a style popular to many.

In Africa the folk music was able to come about through the ranges of their own culture and other foreign influences. The music in Africa helps for people to gather together to find a strengthening in the fabric of their community. It is able to reinforce the commitment to support one another and the community. Here, folk music was seen farther than the purposes of entertainment, it was more about how people would truly have to stand together to survive. Seeing how the music was able to be created and how the folk music was able to flourish within people, it created a calming atmosphere.

As time passed, change occurred with their own forces of colonization, independence, and globalization. Since this changed happened, there was a massive change on how the folk music was able to influence the people of the region. There was a new infusion of instruments, musical styles, and other forms of genres that came over from outside of Africa. The African slave trade and migration was also a massive changed that happened during this time as the music and dance forms of the people changed depending on where they landed.

For the idea of defining the traditional music of Africa, there are many characteristics of Africa that are able to encompass the ways of colonization by the other European countries. Both ways, there was still the existence of tradition within Africa and there continued to be traditions for the reasons behind the folk music. It is about how music was always an important part of the African ethnic life as it was paired with celebrations of childbirth, marriage, hunting, and even other forms of political activities. Many other cultures in Africa would use music through both song and dance to remove evil spirits. These same cultures would be able to use song and dance to give resect to their ancestors, the good spirits, and the dead. For example, there are many types of work songs, ceremonial songs, religious music, and other forms of courtly music that was performed at royal courts. None of these songs were ever truly performed outside of their intended use.

While there were many different cultures and many different forms of diversity in music in Africa, there were common traits that can be seen in order to show how folk music was able to be created on an overall level. One of these common traits is that there was always an emphasis placed more on the rhythm of the song rather than the melody or the harmony. The use of repetition in the songs was able to create a longer rhythm for people to enjoy as they would be able to go off of the improvisation built from the people around them. These forms of African music were mainly performed by a group of musicians that were normally employing other people for polyphony, polyrhythm, and for simply a conversational style of music that would be able to have people together as one group.

For the form of the music they use, it was called ostinato. This form is known to be a repeat of short musical phrases that are later on paired with melodic rhythmic patterns. For example, a main singer will sing a verse then background singers will repeat that same verse back in response. In this form, two or more melodies are able to be combines in order to form a larger sectional formation. The contrast in the song is able to be achieved through the dance or musical movements of the songs. The people in the background of the song were able to create a sense of balance for people to see as they would put themselves in a certain act for people to see. This act and these movements would be repeated several times as well.

The rhythm structure of the songs is the main part that is able to set apart the African musical tradition from the others. There are four basic elements that are able to characterize the rhythmic structure of the songs: equal pulse base, metric time arrangement, specific organizing principle, and an exact starting point. The specific organizing principle is able to unify the diversity of the rhythmic patterns together as the exact starting point is able to provide the appropriate starting point for the people to see. This is for both the crowd and the singers themselves to ensure that everyone is beginning on the same note and melody together.

In South America, the folk music is going to come from the wide margin of Latin America music because of the colonization of the Spanish and the Portuguese. Since this happened, the traditions became mixed and there was a large shift in the influences that were able to shift through the region overall. Either way, there was still dance, religion, art, and music to be seen as an important factor of the land.

Music was able to make up the daily lives of the people. There was music for agricultural labor, marketing animals, building houses, weddings, funerals, etc. Since there were songs for many different types of occasions, there were also many different dances that came about. The instruments used in South America were the pan pipes, flutes, rattles, drums, and the guitar. The most famous type of music that many people are able to recognize quickly is salsa music. Even though it is mainly a characteristic that can over from the regions of Peru, it still became a part of the culture.

Here, one of the most important sites for music to take place was at a cathedral. Their music was used for rituals and celebrations. It was taken from the ideas of prehistoric history to show how people are able to carry their own culture for many generations. The missionaries that were there were able to introduce European music and dance styles to people as they were then able to be an aid to the conversion of people to their religion. By helping to show the type of melody that would be able to draw people in, they were able to get more people to see things from their perspective. They were able to show people that a smooth melody can do more than simply please a crowd.

The teaching of the Catholic religious music went through as a smooth melody and a chant for people to follow. This was done in order to show the new people that entered the church that they all have the ability to join in. There are scales for the rhythm that are used to give what is called a 'church mode'. These are simple rhythmic and melodic parts of the song that are able to spread the ideas of their own beliefs. It came out to be known as a strong European foundation that later on encouraged the folk music traditions that people knew about in the growing generations. For example, the song 'canon' was put into different Indian songs. The mix of the songs became a large part of a three part harmonic sing system done by the choir. Eventually, this became the norm for people to follow as they came for the social aspect of the public, the religious aspect of the church, and then the emotional aspect of the songs.

Quiz:

Question 1: In Europe, what creation allowed for folk music to be spread faster?

Question 2: The idea of the Strophic Form was used in folk music and what other form of art in Europe?

Question 3: What kind of folk music in Asia could be compared to the popularity of today's rock n' roll?

Question 4: What was the most important site for music to take place at in South America?

Conclusion

Modern music is continuing to develop and expand with no end in sight, but often seems to go back to visit its roots in the early blues music. With Classical music making a big comeback, it sometimes seems the gap between the two at times reduces and maybe one-day may be filled.

Thank you for reading this book, I hope you enjoyed reading it and got some value from it. Down below are the answers to each of the quiz questions:

Chapter 1:

Question 1: Word painting is when there is more of an importance on the words or lyrics of a song rather than the instruments being used. Question 2: The printing press. Question 3: Beethoven.

Chapter 2:

Question 1: The Baroque Period (1600-1750). Question 2: The Total Art Work. Question 3: Johann Sebastian Bach. Question 4: Richard Wagner. Question 5: The leitmotif.

Chapter 3:

Question 1: Southern plantations through a multitude of chants, drum music, country dance music, chants, and hymns. Question 2: New Orleans.

Chapter 4:

Question 1: Elvis Aaron Presley.

Chapter 5:

Question 1: poor white people. Question 2: rock n' roll.

Chapter 6:

Question 1: musique concrete. Question 2: designated electronic music.

Chapter 7:

Question 1: Thriller. Question 2: Singing and piano playing.

Chapter 8:

Question 1: bone flute. Question 2: Middle to Late Bronze Age. Question 3: Celebrations and rituals.

Chapter 9:

Question 1: True, Question 2: Dopamine.

Chapter 10:

Question 1: Cultural, Moral, Emotional, and Political. Question 2: People would have a difference of opinion.

Chapter 11:

Question 1: The invention of printing. Question 2: poetry. Question 3: Pakistani. Question 4: The Cathedral.

Made in the USA
Monee, IL
22 March 2023

30371919R00036